EMMANUEL JOSEPH

Whispers of Wisdom: Daily Reflections for a Mindful Life

Copyright © 2025 by Emmanuel Joseph

All rights reserved. No part of this publication may be reproduced, stored or transmitted in any form or by any means, electronic, mechanical, photocopying, recording, scanning, or otherwise without written permission from the publisher. It is illegal to copy this book, post it to a website, or distribute it by any other means without permission.

First edition

*This book was professionally typeset on Reedsy.
Find out more at reedsy.com*

Contents

1. Chapter 1: Embracing the Present Moment — 1
2. Chapter 2: Finding Stillness Amidst Chaos — 2
3. Chapter 3: Cultivating Compassion — 3
4. Chapter 4: Letting Go of Judgment — 4
5. Chapter 5: Nurturing a Growth Mindset — 5
6. Chapter 6: Building Meaningful Connections — 6
7. Chapter 7: Practicing Mindful Eating — 7
8. Chapter 8: Embracing Change and Impermanence — 8
9. Chapter 9: Living with Purpose and Intention — 9
10. Chapter 10: Cultivating Joy and Positivity — 10
11. Chapter 11: Creating a Mindful Daily Routine — 11
12. Chapter 12: Sustaining a Mindful Life — 12
13. Chapter 13: Mindfulness in Communication — 13
14. Chapter 14: Mindful Technology Use — 14
15. Chapter 15: Mindfulness in the Workplace — 15
16. Chapter 16: Mindfulness in Nature — 16
17. Chapter 17: Mindfulness and Creativity — 17
18. Chapter 18: Mindful Self-Care — 18

1

Chapter 1: Embracing the Present Moment

Paragraph 1: In our fast-paced world, it's easy to get caught up in the hustle and bustle, constantly thinking about the next task or worry. However, mindfulness invites us to slow down and truly experience the present moment. By being fully present, we can find joy in the simple things and appreciate the beauty around us.

Paragraph 2: One way to embrace the present moment is through mindful breathing. Take a few deep breaths and focus on the sensation of the air entering and leaving your body. This simple practice can ground you in the here and now, allowing you to let go of stress and anxiety.

Paragraph 3: Another powerful tool for mindfulness is gratitude. Take a moment each day to reflect on the things you are grateful for. This practice shifts your focus from what you lack to what you have, fostering a sense of contentment and happiness.

Paragraph 4: Finally, practice being fully engaged in whatever you are doing. Whether it's eating a meal, having a conversation, or taking a walk, give your full attention to the experience. This not only enhances your enjoyment but also deepens your connection to the present moment.

2

Chapter 2: Finding Stillness Amidst Chaos

Paragraph 1: Life is often chaotic, filled with noise and distractions. Yet, amidst the chaos, there is a stillness within us that we can tap into through mindfulness. This inner stillness is a source of calm and clarity, helping us navigate the ups and downs of life with greater ease.

Paragraph 2: Meditation is a powerful practice for accessing this inner stillness. By setting aside a few minutes each day to sit quietly and focus on your breath, you can cultivate a sense of peace and centeredness. Over time, this practice can transform your relationship with stress and anxiety.

Paragraph 3: Another way to find stillness is through mindful movement. Whether it's yoga, tai chi, or simply a walk in nature, moving mindfully helps you connect with your body and quiet your mind. Pay attention to the sensations of your body and the rhythm of your movements, allowing yourself to fully immerse in the experience.

Paragraph 4: Lastly, create moments of stillness throughout your day. Take a few deep breaths before responding to a stressful email, or pause for a moment of silence before starting a new task. These small moments of stillness can make a big difference in your overall sense of calm and well-being.

3

Chapter 3: Cultivating Compassion

Paragraph 1: Compassion is a key component of mindfulness, both for ourselves and others. By cultivating compassion, we can approach life with greater kindness and understanding, reducing suffering and fostering connection.

Paragraph 2: Self-compassion is the practice of being kind and gentle with yourself, especially during difficult times. Instead of harsh self-criticism, offer yourself words of encouragement and support. Remember that everyone makes mistakes and experiences challenges—it's part of being human.

Paragraph 3: Extending compassion to others involves recognizing their humanity and suffering. Practice active listening, offering your full attention and empathy. Even small acts of kindness, like a smile or a helping hand, can make a significant impact on someone's day.

Paragraph 4: Lastly, cultivate a sense of universal compassion. Recognize that all beings, regardless of their differences, experience joy and suffering. By developing a compassionate heart, we can contribute to a more compassionate and interconnected world.

4

Chapter 4: Letting Go of Judgment

Paragraph 1: Judgment often clouds our perception and hinders our ability to connect with ourselves and others. Mindfulness teaches us to observe without judgment, allowing us to see things as they are and respond with greater clarity and compassion.

Paragraph 2: One way to let go of judgment is to practice mindful awareness. Notice when judgment arises in your thoughts, and instead of reacting, simply observe it. Acknowledge the judgment without getting caught up in it, and gently redirect your focus to the present moment.

Paragraph 3: Another practice is to cultivate a sense of curiosity. Instead of labeling experiences or people as good or bad, approach them with an open mind and a sense of wonder. This shift in perspective can help you see things in a new light and appreciate the richness of life.

Paragraph 4: Letting go of judgment also involves self-acceptance. Embrace your imperfections and recognize that you are a work in progress. By accepting yourself as you are, you create space for growth and transformation.

5

Chapter 5: Nurturing a Growth Mindset

Paragraph 1: A growth mindset is the belief that our abilities and intelligence can be developed through effort and learning. Mindfulness supports a growth mindset by encouraging us to embrace challenges and view setbacks as opportunities for growth.

Paragraph 2: One way to nurture a growth mindset is to practice self-reflection. Take time to reflect on your experiences, identifying areas where you have grown and areas where you can continue to improve. This practice helps you stay focused on your goals and motivated to keep growing.

Paragraph 3: Another important aspect of a growth mindset is resilience. Cultivate resilience by developing healthy coping strategies, such as seeking support from others, practicing self-care, and maintaining a positive outlook. Resilience helps you bounce back from setbacks and keep moving forward.

Paragraph 4: Finally, celebrate your progress and successes, no matter how small. Acknowledge the effort and dedication you have put into your growth journey, and take pride in your accomplishments. This positive reinforcement fuels your motivation and confidence to continue growing.

6

Chapter 6: Building Meaningful Connections

Paragraph 1: Meaningful connections with others are essential for our well-being and happiness. Mindfulness helps us build and nurture these connections by fostering presence, empathy, and authentic communication.

Paragraph 2: One way to build meaningful connections is through active listening. Give your full attention to the person you are speaking with, without interrupting or thinking about your response. This practice shows respect and genuine interest, strengthening your bond with others.

Paragraph 3: Empathy is another key component of meaningful connections. Practice putting yourself in others' shoes, understanding their feelings and perspectives. This empathetic approach helps you connect on a deeper level and respond with compassion and support.

Paragraph 4: Lastly, practice authentic communication. Be open and honest in your interactions, sharing your thoughts and feelings with vulnerability. Authenticity fosters trust and intimacy, creating a strong foundation for meaningful relationships.

7

Chapter 7: Practicing Mindful Eating

Paragraph 1: Eating is not just about nourishing our bodies—it's an opportunity to cultivate mindfulness and deepen our connection with food. Mindful eating involves paying full attention to the experience of eating, from the flavors and textures to the sensations in our body.

Paragraph 2: One way to practice mindful eating is to slow down and savor each bite. Take small bites, chew thoroughly, and notice the different flavors and textures. This practice not only enhances your enjoyment of food but also helps you become more aware of your hunger and fullness cues.

Paragraph 3: Another aspect of mindful eating is to eat without distractions. Avoid watching TV, using your phone, or working while eating. Instead, focus solely on the act of eating and the sensory experience it provides. This helps you develop a more conscious and intentional relationship with food.

Paragraph 4: Lastly, cultivate gratitude for your food. Take a moment before eating to appreciate where your food comes from, the effort it took to prepare it, and the nourishment it provides. This practice fosters a sense of appreciation and connection to the food you eat.

Chapter 8: Embracing Change and Impermanence

Paragraph 1: Change is an inevitable part of life, and mindfulness teaches us to embrace it with grace and acceptance. By recognizing the impermanent nature of all things, we can navigate life's transitions with greater ease and resilience.

Paragraph 2: One way to embrace change is to practice acceptance. Instead of resisting or fearing change, acknowledge it as a natural part of life. Acceptance doesn't mean passive resignation; it means recognizing reality and finding ways to adapt and move forward.

Paragraph 3: Another practice is to focus on the present moment. When faced with change, it's easy to get caught up in worries about the future. By staying grounded in the present, you can approach change with a clearer mind and a calmer heart.

Paragraph 4: Lastly, cultivate a sense of curiosity and openness to change. View change as an opportunity for growth and new experiences. This mindset helps you stay flexible and resilient, ready to embrace whatever comes your way.

9

Chapter 9: Living with Purpose and Intention

Paragraph 1: Living with purpose and intention means aligning your actions with your values and goals. Mindfulness helps you cultivate a deeper sense of purpose by encouraging self-reflection and intentional living.

Paragraph 2: One way to live with purpose is to identify your core values. Reflect on what matters most to you and how you can incorporate these values into your daily life. This practice helps you stay true to yourself and make decisions that align with your beliefs.

Paragraph 3: Another practice is to set intentional goals. Instead of setting vague or unrealistic goals, create specific and achievable ones that align with your values and aspirations. This approach helps you stay focused and motivated on your path.

Paragraph 4: Lastly, practice mindful decision-making. Take time to consider your options and the potential impact of your choices. By making decisions with awareness and intention

By making decisions with awareness and intention, you can ensure that your actions align with your purpose and values. This practice empowers you to live a life that is both meaningful and fulfilling.

Chapter 10: Cultivating Joy and Positivity

Paragraph 1: Joy and positivity are essential for a mindful life. By cultivating these qualities, we can enhance our overall well-being and approach life with a more positive outlook. Mindfulness helps us recognize and savor the moments of joy in our daily lives.

Paragraph 2: One way to cultivate joy is to practice gratitude. Take time each day to reflect on the things you are grateful for, whether big or small. This practice shifts your focus to the positive aspects of your life and fosters a sense of contentment and happiness.

Paragraph 3: Another practice is to engage in activities that bring you joy. Whether it's a hobby, spending time with loved ones, or simply enjoying a beautiful sunset, make time for the things that make you happy. These moments of joy can uplift your spirits and create lasting memories.

Paragraph 4: Lastly, cultivate a positive mindset by focusing on the good in every situation. Even in challenging times, look for the silver lining and the lessons you can learn. This optimistic approach helps you navigate life's ups and downs with resilience and grace.

11

Chapter 11: Creating a Mindful Daily Routine

Paragraph 1: A mindful daily routine can help you start and end your day with intention and purpose. By incorporating mindfulness practices into your daily routine, you can create a sense of balance and harmony in your life.

Paragraph 2: Start your day with a few moments of mindfulness. This could be a brief meditation, a few deep breaths, or simply setting an intention for the day. This practice helps you begin your day with a clear and focused mind.

Paragraph 3: Throughout the day, take mindful breaks. Step away from your work or responsibilities for a few minutes to stretch, breathe, or simply be present. These mindful pauses can refresh your mind and body, enhancing your productivity and well-being.

Paragraph 4: End your day with a mindfulness practice, such as reflecting on the events of the day, expressing gratitude, or practicing a relaxation technique. This helps you unwind and prepare for a restful night's sleep, ensuring you wake up refreshed and ready for the new day.

12

Chapter 12: Sustaining a Mindful Life

Paragraph 1: Sustaining a mindful life is an ongoing journey that requires commitment and practice. By integrating mindfulness into your daily life, you can continue to cultivate peace, clarity, and purpose.

Paragraph 2: One way to sustain mindfulness is to stay connected to your practice. Whether it's through meditation, mindful breathing, or other practices, make mindfulness a regular part of your routine. This consistency helps reinforce the benefits of mindfulness and keeps you grounded.

Paragraph 3: Another important aspect is to stay open to learning and growth. Continuously explore new mindfulness practices and approaches, and be open to adapting your practice as your needs and circumstances change. This openness helps you stay engaged and motivated on your mindfulness journey.

Paragraph 4: Lastly, remember that mindfulness is a lifelong practice. Be patient and compassionate with yourself, recognizing that there will be ups and downs along the way. By staying committed to your practice and embracing the journey, you can live a mindful life filled with wisdom, peace, and joy.

Chapter 13: Mindfulness in Communication

Paragraph 1: Mindful communication is about being fully present and attentive in our interactions with others. It involves listening deeply, speaking with intention, and being aware of our own thoughts and emotions as we communicate.

Paragraph 2: One way to practice mindful communication is to listen without interrupting. Give the speaker your full attention, and resist the urge to jump in with your own thoughts or responses. This creates a space for genuine understanding and connection.

Paragraph 3: Another aspect of mindful communication is to speak with intention. Choose your words carefully, and aim to express yourself clearly and authentically. Avoid speaking out of anger or frustration, and instead, communicate with compassion and respect.

Paragraph 4: Lastly, be aware of your own emotions and reactions during conversations. Notice how you feel and what thoughts arise, and use this awareness to respond mindfully rather than reactively. This approach fosters healthier and more meaningful interactions.

14

Chapter 14: Mindful Technology Use

Paragraph 1: Technology is a significant part of our lives, but it can also be a source of distraction and stress. Mindful technology use involves being intentional and aware of how we interact with our devices, and finding a balance that supports our well-being.

Paragraph 2: One way to practice mindful technology use is to set boundaries. Designate specific times for checking emails, social media, and other online activities, and stick to these boundaries. This helps prevent mindless scrolling and reduces the impact of digital overload.

Paragraph 3: Another practice is to create tech-free zones or times. For example, make mealtimes or certain rooms in your home free of devices. This encourages face-to-face interactions and allows you to be fully present in your environment.

Paragraph 4: Lastly, be mindful of your digital consumption. Choose content that enriches your life and aligns with your values, and avoid getting caught up in negative or superficial information. This intentional approach to technology helps you use it in a way that enhances your well-being.

15

Chapter 15: Mindfulness in the Workplace

Paragraph 1: Bringing mindfulness into the workplace can improve your focus, productivity, and overall job satisfaction. By being present and intentional in your work, you can navigate the demands of your job with greater ease and resilience.

Paragraph 2: One way to practice mindfulness at work is to start your day with a clear intention. Take a few moments to set a positive and focused mindset before diving into your tasks. This helps you approach your work with clarity and purpose.

Paragraph 3: Another practice is to take mindful breaks. Step away from your desk for a few minutes to stretch, breathe, or simply be present. These breaks can refresh your mind and body, enhancing your productivity and creativity.

Paragraph 4: Lastly, practice mindful communication with your colleagues. Listen actively, speak with intention, and be aware of your own emotions and reactions. This fosters a positive and supportive work environment, promoting collaboration and well-being.

16

Chapter 16: Mindfulness in Nature

Paragraph 1: Nature has a profound ability to ground and inspire us. By practicing mindfulness in nature, we can deepen our connection to the natural world and find a sense of peace and wonder.

Paragraph 2: One way to practice mindfulness in nature is to engage your senses. Notice the sights, sounds, smells, and sensations around you, and allow yourself to be fully present in the experience. This sensory awareness enhances your appreciation of the natural world.

Paragraph 3: Another practice is to spend time in nature regularly. Whether it's a walk in the park, a hike in the mountains, or simply sitting in your backyard, make time to connect with nature. This regular immersion in nature supports your overall well-being.

Paragraph 4: Lastly, practice gratitude for the natural world. Take a moment to appreciate the beauty and abundance of nature, and reflect on your connection to the earth. This practice fosters a sense of wonder and respect for the environment.

17

Chapter 17: Mindfulness and Creativity

Paragraph 1: Mindfulness and creativity go hand in hand. By being present and open, we can tap into our creative potential and express ourselves more authentically. Mindfulness helps us overcome creative blocks and find inspiration in the moment.

Paragraph 2: One way to cultivate mindfulness and creativity is to create a dedicated space for your creative practice. Set aside a time and place where you can fully immerse yourself in your creative endeavors, free from distractions.

Paragraph 3: Another practice is to approach your creative work with curiosity and openness. Instead of focusing on the end result, allow yourself to explore and experiment. This playful and non-judgmental approach fosters creativity and innovation.

Paragraph 4: Lastly, use mindfulness to overcome creative blocks. When you feel stuck, take a few moments to breathe deeply and reconnect with the present moment. This can help you release tension and open up to new ideas and possibilities.

18

Chapter 18: Mindful Self-Care

Paragraph 1: Self-care is essential for maintaining our physical, emotional, and mental well-being. Mindful self-care involves being aware of our needs and intentionally taking steps to nourish and care for ourselves.

Paragraph 2: One way to practice mindful self-care is to tune into your body. Notice how you feel and what your body needs, whether it's rest, nourishment, or movement. Respond to these needs with kindness and compassion.

Paragraph 3: Another practice is to create a self-care routine. Set aside regular time for activities that replenish and rejuvenate you, such as meditation, exercise, or creative pursuits. This consistent self-care routine supports your overall well-being.

Paragraph 4: Lastly, practice self-compassion. Be gentle with yourself, especially during challenging times. Acknowledge your efforts and progress, and offer yourself the same kindness and support you would offer a friend. This self-compassion fosters a healthy and balanced approach to self-care.

Book Description

Dive into a transformative journey with **"Whispers of Wisdom: Daily Reflections for a Mindful Life"**. This captivating collection offers twelve insightful chapters designed to bring mindfulness into your everyday life. Each chapter brims with thoughtful reflections and practical advice to help you embrace the present moment, find stillness amid chaos, cultivate

CHAPTER 18: MINDFUL SELF-CARE

compassion, and nurture meaningful connections.

Discover the art of mindful living through practices such as mindful breathing, gratitude, and authentic communication. Learn to navigate life's challenges with grace and resilience by embracing change, fostering a growth mindset, and practicing mindful self-care. Whether you're seeking to enhance your creativity, build a mindful daily routine, or connect deeply with nature, this book provides the guidance you need.

"Whispers of Wisdom" is more than just a book—it's a companion on your journey toward a life filled with purpose, clarity, and joy. Each reflection serves as a gentle reminder to slow down, be present, and live with intention. Perfect for anyone looking to cultivate mindfulness and enrich their daily life, this book is your gateway to a more peaceful and fulfilling existence.

www.ingramcontent.com/pod-product-compliance
Lightning Source LLC
LaVergne TN
LVHW020509080526
838202LV00057B/6267